BREAKING THROUGH
a book of poetry

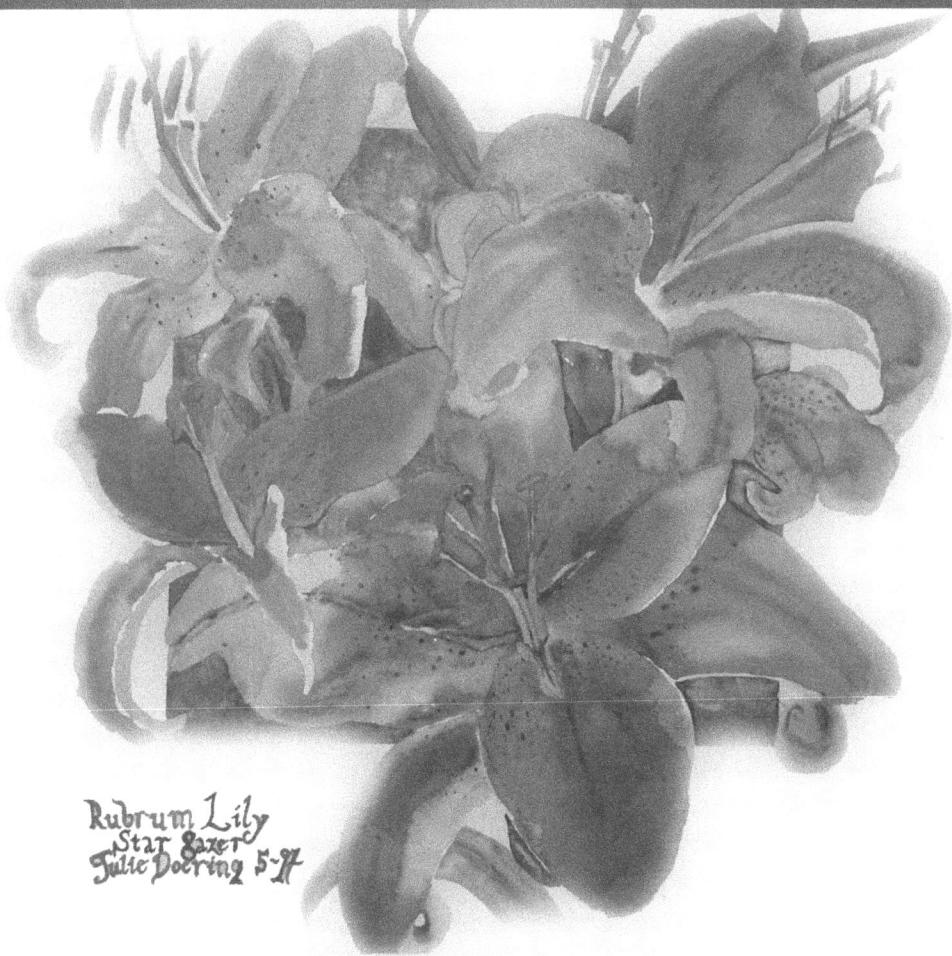

Rubrum Lily
Star Gazer
Julie Doering 5-11

JULIE RENEE DOERING

BREAKING THROUGH

a book of poetry

Limited Edition
Julie Renee Doering

San Francisco, CA
1996

Breaking Through: a book of poetry

ISBN-13: 978-0-9970044-5-8

Gable-Kennedy Publications All Rights Reserved.
PO Box 549
Carmel Valley, California 93924
Info@Julierenee.com

Printed in the U.S.A.

Book design and cover:

Warning – Disclaimer

The purpose of this book is to educate and entertain. The author and/ or publisher does not guarantee that anyone following the techniques, suggestions, tips, ideas or strategies will become successful. The author and/or publisher shall have neither liability nor responsibility to anyone with respect to any loss or damage caused, or alleged to be caused, directly by the information in this book.

Endorsement – Disclaimer

Reference herein to any specific commercial products, process, or service by trade name, trademark, manufacturer, or otherwise, in no manner endorses or sponsors the products, processes or offerings.

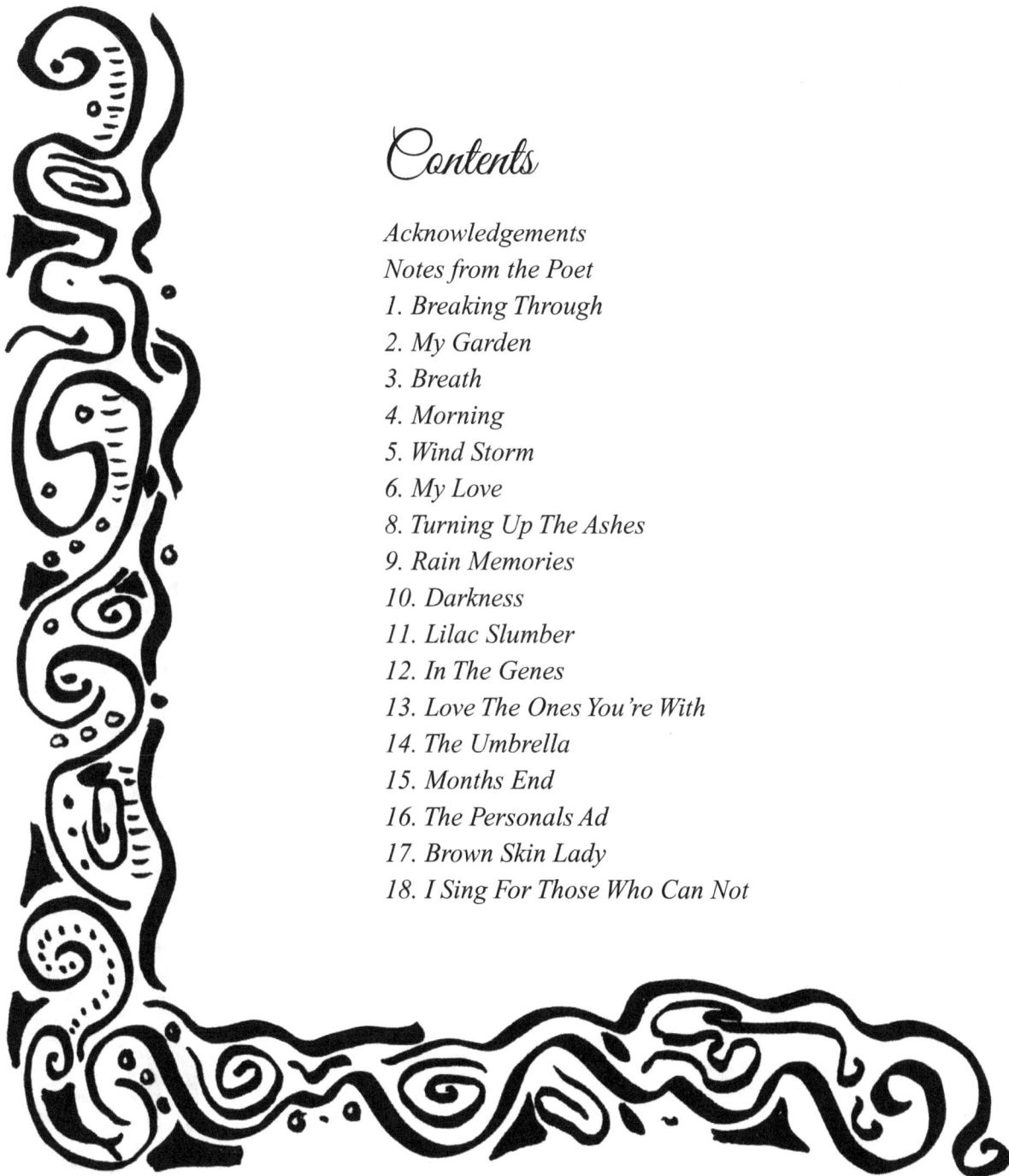

Contents

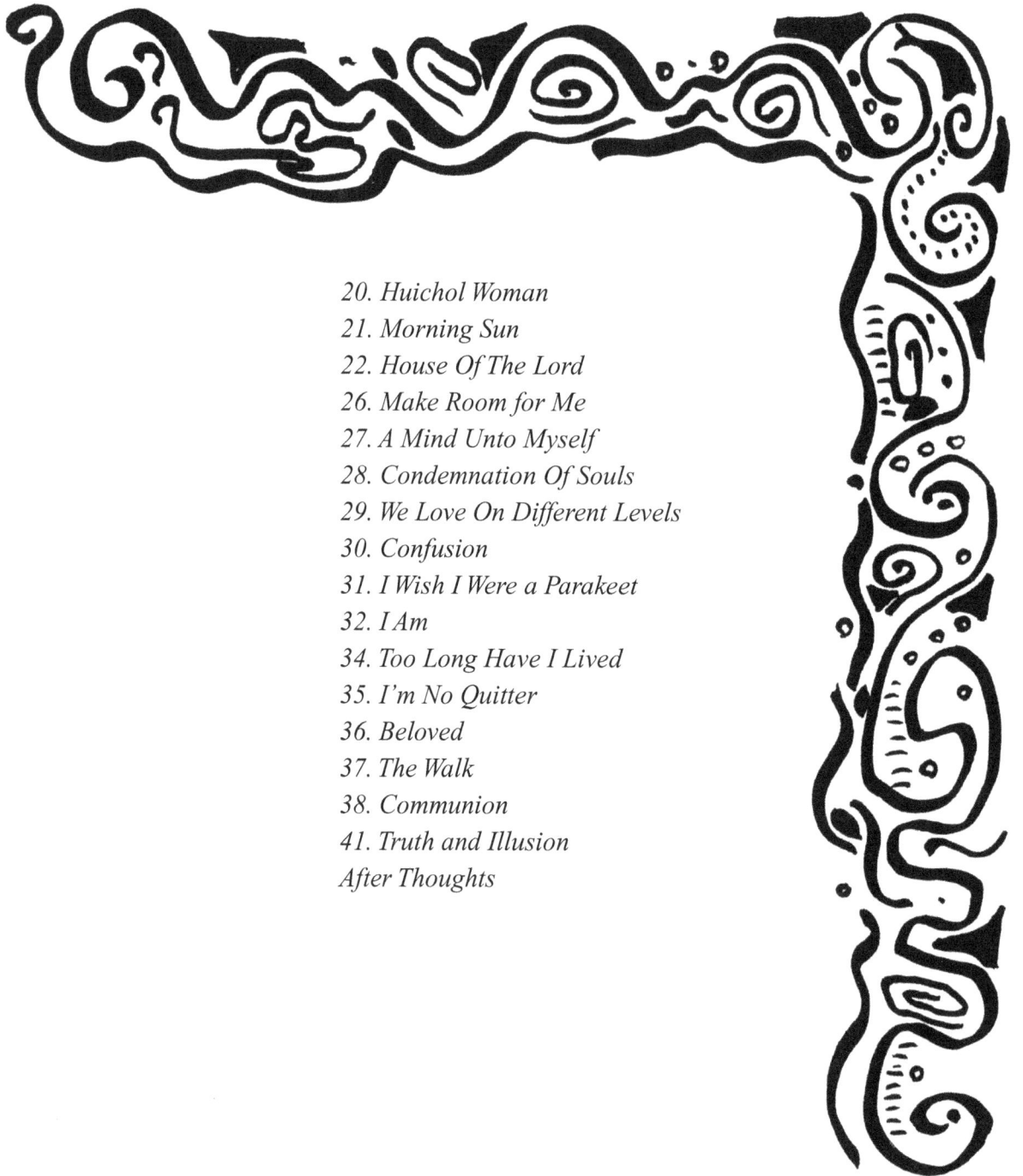

Acknowledgements

I am grateful to so many people who have supported and encouraged me along the way. Jean Hentges, Hannah Shirah, Eileen Silon, Rebecca Jamison, Michael George and Jacques-Marie Lasseau each of whom has been extraordinary. Special thanks to Mary Mattledge for teaching me the art of book making. Warmest thanks go to my counselors Dr. Ulrich Berg and Julia Shumelda who have served as spiritual and emotional mentors through some fairly rocky moments. Love to my beautiful children Britta, Rebeccah and Peter. Any most importantly my unending gratitude to my angels, guides and creator for the gift of life, love and courage.

Julie Renee Doering
San Francisco, California, 1996

Notes From the Poet

I walked the Labyrinth today at Grace Cathedral. My walk through the winds and curves of the circular meditation path, matched perfectly with the path of my life. In the Labyrinth you walk a path that leads you closer and farther away from your center, finally ending up in the center, which in this sacred space is a flower, resembling a crown. As I walked the Labyrinth, I found myself crying, at times in life I have felt so far from my center, then suddenly without warning, I am close again. It's a perfect metaphor for life, walking the curves and turns, going forward and backward, not knowing if you're still on the same path to your center or not, but following the meditation, because there is no other way.

This poetry is the flow of my life in some small way. The struggles I have had with physical illness and deep depression, along with the observing eye and stubborn determination that can yell out, I'm no quitter. It is my hope that these few select pieces will give you a sense of pilgrimage along the continuing path way to my Labyrinths Center.

Thank you so much for your interest in this work, though I have been published numerous times, this is my first solo effort.

May you be blessed as you walk your own lives meditation

With Appreciation
Julie

Breaking Through

Rain keeps falling.
I feel God grieving with me.
Crying the tears of Loss,
we wash away the stains of absent love.

Our tears nourish a fertile ground.
We ready the earth and her seeds
For their inevitable duty.

Bringing forth new life,
again and again.
Each time with no less pain,
the sprout breaks through
her protective shell.

The seedling grows, flowers,
and at long last, bares the fruits of love.
She offers her fruit freely to anyone
who would accept this gift.

Breaking through is a painful thing,
with no guarantee of success.
Yet the seedling must forge ahead,
its quest for life too strong to repress.

My Garden

My garden is a quiet place,
I work it lush and fine.
My plants are rows of circles,
that weave their way through time.

Breath

I cry the tears of lost love
…and breath…
I let you in.
All I hoped for is gone,
Yet, you are here loving me.
I am in need of your devotion.
…Waves of emotion…
I feel unable to hide a moment longer.
Feelings of loneliness surround me
like gray fog on a cold day.
I weary of being strong and brave
in this dreary climate.
You offer me your willingness.
I am grateful.
…Breath…
I inhale you into my being.

Morning

I felt your cheek rub against mine.
I lay joyously in your arms.
Your soft inner thigh gently caressed my waist.
The boat gently rocked,
while the sunlight beamed through the portals.
We snuggle in warm blankets,
spun wool, woven by your skilled hands.
In my deep exhaustion, I felt love and safety.
As I drifted off in sleep you devotedly held me
for an eternal hour.
I rolled deeper into you.
My cheek caressed the hollow of your neck.
You held me even closer,
As if we had melted into one being.

Wind Storm

The wind is blowing.
My hands are cold.
I've wrapped my feet
in stockings old.

A storm may come.
It's hard to tell.
We've revelled in this day
far from hell.

The sun shines bright.
We rest on the boat.
Tied secure and fast,
we stay afloat.

The light still shines,
Though howling go the winds.
Three boats tethered tight,
Off Angel Island, by the bend.

My Love

My life exists in your loving.
Your face is the bright sun rising out of the night.
Your familiar touch, like warm flannel sheets in winter.
Eternity is our love.

I feel gratitude for those who have shaped you.
I am deeply appreciative of those who have loved you.
Yet as I reflect back on the hundreds of stories you've told,
I've not heard stories of your deepest loving.

You have not spoken of total love and acceptance,
even if just for a moment.

Is that the story we will create?

Will that be the story you tell twenty years from now
when you reflect on our first time together?

My life has changed so, since our love was planted
My soil has been well fertilized from stagnant,
rotted love gone sour.

There are times when I am frightened of you.
Your moods, confused.
These are the times you don't feel me loving you.
I am still there.

And when we are securely connected,
I speak my mind freely.

Turning Up The Ashes

I thought there would be more.
I am left with an emptiness.
Like ash after the roaring blaze is long extinguished,
desperately I search for the remnants of a spark
to rekindle my fire.

Searching goes on in vain.
I recognize ash is sacred.
Complete in its existence.
I hunger for fires of passion to restore the
brilliant flame to me.

One cold day you'll look out your window and
find me still,
turning up the ashes with my cane.
Restlessly seeking an unanswerable quest,
to find the life we once knew.

I remember you my beloved.
In my memories live the searing flames
of the love we bore.
Our glory shall light my long dark night.

Rain Memories

A tree.
The grass.
The fresh smell of rain.
I remember the scent of an angle worm.
Gray skies.
Sad days.
Wishing to play.
The occasional escape!
Ecstasy in flooded streets!
Hoards of neighbor kids splash on.
The goulashes.
The rain slickers.
My wet head,
covered with a favorite cotton scarf.
The silly plastic bonnet
grama gave me to wear.
Drop on me misty rain.
Remind me of where I came!

Darkness

Darkness
Can't see.
Feeling darkness,
emerging in me.

Hiding
Where am I now?
Behind boxes,
listening to screams.

Frightened.
Thuds.
Fist hitting flesh.
Crys.
Someone's in pain.
I am safe.

Awareness.
Closing off sounds.
Despair.
Ease.
No sound at all.

Invisible.
Floating free.
Unreachable.
Empty.
Quiet.

I have become nothing.

Lilac Slumber

I lay under the lilacs.
I am twenty-four.
My world is at an end.

I cry the tears of a dead marriage.
I cry the tears of a dying body.
I cry the tears of a mother,
who will not see her children
grow to adulthood.

The sky is cloudy.
I can vaguely hear my daughter's quiet sobs,
from the distant farm house porch I call home.

So little life in me,
I cannot respond.

The clouds move on
as I lay in the green grass,
hardly breathing.

In The Genes

What is a family?
A genetic strand,
that hurls us together
linking us hand in hand?
Or an intellectual tick,
that makes us click?
Our shared past,
Does that make us last?
Could it be our choice?
Do we have a voice?
Could we be a family
without a natal tree?
Is being together with love
the "family" sanctioned from above?
Are families the true friends
who we rely on and depend?
Can I, by myself, choose to make a bond,
and find it to live on and on?
Or is the support from friends to come and go?
On this question, I must know.
If I love you as my clan today,
can I count on you to be in my life next May?
Can I trust you not to leave?
Can I trust you with my love?
Can I trust?

Love The Ones You're With

The answers are not in the questions you ask.
Sense cannot be made of them.
You must ask new questions, till the answers bring you
divine peace and contentment.

Why hope, when all you need awaits your call?
Why grieve when life has given you more than your share?

Be happy with the simple things,
the tender touch of a loved one as you sleep,
the caress of misty rain on your check, and
the call of the ocean waves beckoning you to dance.

I am not convinced you have one reason, at this moment
to feel anything other than ecstasy, unless, you will it so.

Meditate on the petals of an orchid, or the spry dandelion.
Breathe in the salty ocean air.
Thank the heavens for the stars it shares with you,
and, love the ones you're with.

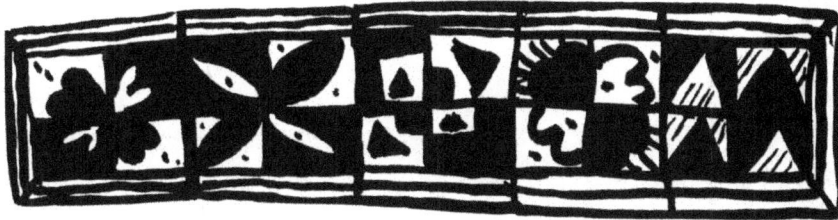

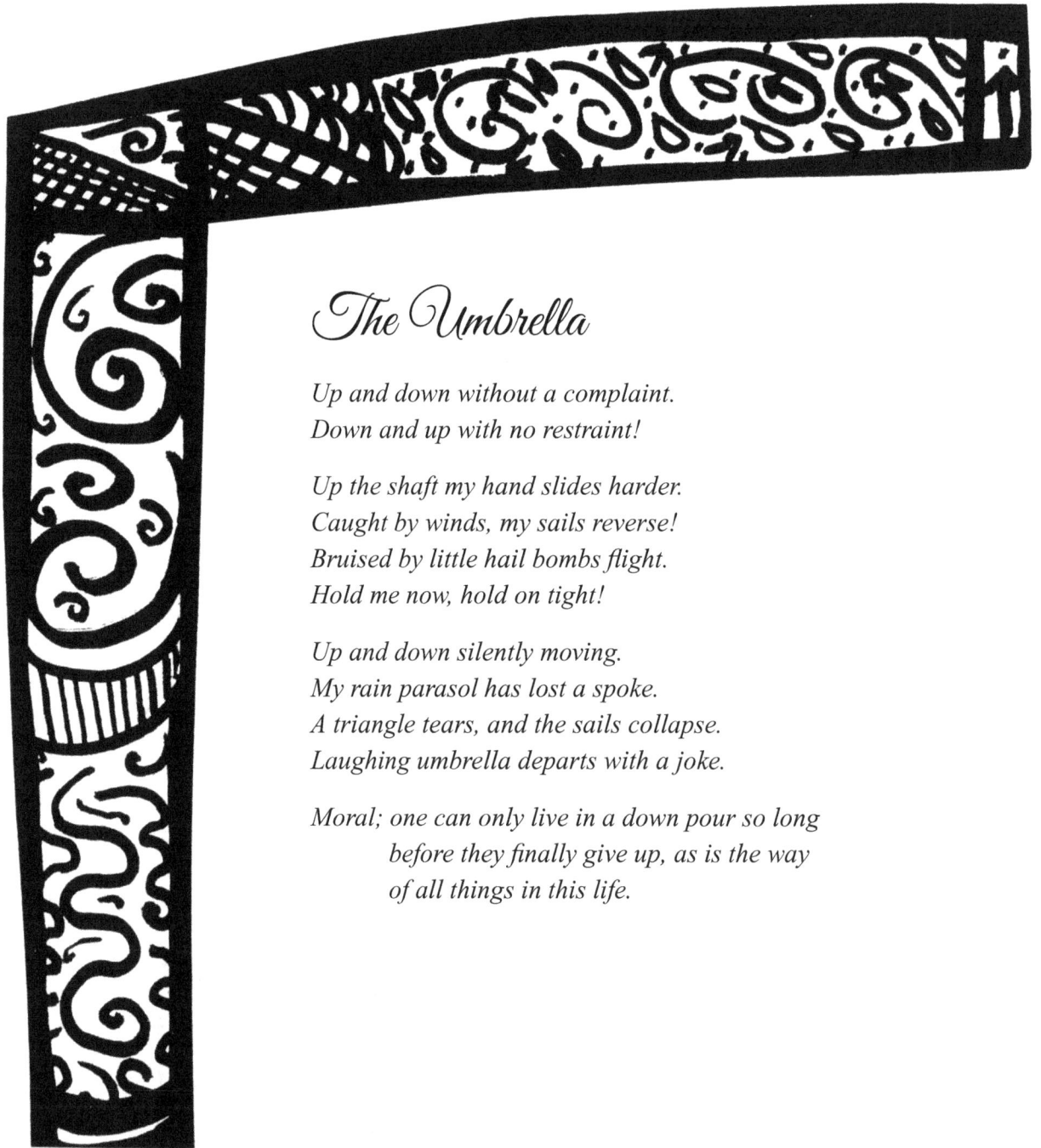

The Umbrella

Up and down without a complaint.
Down and up with no restraint!

Up the shaft my hand slides harder.
Caught by winds, my sails reverse!
Bruised by little hail bombs flight.
Hold me now, hold on tight!

Up and down silently moving.
My rain parasol has lost a spoke.
A triangle tears, and the sails collapse.
Laughing umbrella departs with a joke.

Moral; one can only live in a down pour so long
      before they finally give up, as is the way
         of all things in this life.

Months End

I am cold and tired.
I travel the familiar bus ride home,
complete with the inevitable screeches and bumps.
It's been a long hard month.
I'm glad it's over.

The Personals Ad

Wanted; someone to laugh with.
Must be just the way you are,
don't change a thing.
Wanted; someone to cry with.
No prior experience necessary,
just a willingness to be human.
Wanted; someone of nonspecific
class, color, gender or religion.
Looking for another human being,
being human.
Wanted; someone to share life with.
Must be alive, with a modicum of
hopes, dreams and dissolution's to
balance life.
Wanted; someone who needs touch.
Must be good at giving and receiving.
Wanted; a companion who is sometimes
bright, with the potential for dimness
to share a small place in need of light.
Wanted; someone to love, who will
love me back. Someone who stays
with a good thing, and someone
who enjoys counting the stars.
Wanted; a dream partner. Auditions
to be held next time I sleep. Must be
kind, fund, gentle, spiritual and a true
adventurer at heart.
Responses to previous ads will be taken by voicemail at:
1-976-REA-LOVE

Brown Skinned Lady

I walked down a crowded sidewalk,
my lover and I in firm embrace.
My eyes fell upon a woman amidst the masses.
Old, weak, and sad, she barely saw me.
Crouched low, she curled her little body off the walkway
into the wheel well of an old pick-up truck.
Like a desert floor, long ago moistened by rain,
she wore the cracks of an endless drought on her face.
Our eyes met.
For a moment, I was privy to a glimpse of her soul.
She offered me some small ware.
As I shook no, ever so kindly,
she shrank a portion more.
Not missing a step,
I continued my journey.
My arm entwined in my lovers.
I will remember the moment my eyes embraced
the fragile, brown skinned lady.

I Sing For Those Who Can Not

I sing for those who can not sing.
I cry for those without tears.
I ache to soothe the numb, the still.
I scream for those without fear.

I touch for those who are timid.
I stain for those who remain clean.
I swim naked in the jungle streams,
for the shy, who linger unseen.

I laugh for those in deep sorrow.
I learn for the simple of mind.
Round sacred fires I dance circles,
for the empty, forgotten, divine.

I am a sponge in the ocean,
the essence of healing sublime,
a conduit of energy flows,
out my body and into thine.

I sing because I could not sing.
I recovered my frozen voice.
I cry because I did not cry.
My tears fall freely by choice.

I touch,
I learn,
I dance,
I grow.
I swim naked,
I laugh,
I'm divine.
Bad times will come, good times will go,
right now we stand firm alive.

I love because I was born to love,
I'm tenderness and compassion combined.
I'm rage, fury and power,
awakened in a Christed mind.

I could not feel your burning pain,
if I had not suffered myself.
In weakness I found my power.
In my darkness I merged with the light.

I am with you.
Feel me now.
We are one.

Huichol Woman

She descended from mountains once her refuge.
Survival impossible in a dried-up briar patch.
She emerged from a wild impenetrable land,
to the terrifying jungle of modern humanity.

She was an elder of an exiled tribe.
To the eyes of a passerby, she was just an old woman.
She crouched low and begged, on the diesel polluted walkway.
I witnessed her crying helplessly for her daily bread.

Her appearance was like that of an old flea-bitten dog.
She was a mangy old creature that had been
kicked around once too often.
She wore yards of colorfully woven fabric,
now decaying against the mixture of oil, sweat and dirt,
defecating off her skin.
She had become a tattered rag bag.
The cloth she donned wound its way around her shrinking body
like an old bandage hiding a festering wound.
She wore these rags
as the last visible evidence of her proud heritage.
Her clothes the death shroud honoring her long absent people.

A senseless new breed of humanity
has driven her tribe deep into the uninhabitable swamps.
Scattered them into the rocky places
where they hope to avoid the inevitable....

Extinction.

Morning Sun

I am the morning sun.
I break open the dark egg of night.
I shine through the longest day.
I die with the end of light.

A faithful friend, I am.
Each day I'm born again.
I encourage you on and brighten your way.
Depend on me every dawn.

I am the soul-ar panel of life.
I wrap you in a blanket of love.
My fires scorch fiercely on high.
Down here, I'm gentle as a dove.

The House Of The Lord

Rain beat hard on my window pane,
like lost hands, pounding on glass.
A icy shiver bolted through my spine,
announcing the coming of homeless demons,
habitués of days past.

Protecting myself from dark apparitions,
I pulled hard the weighted layers of comforters to my body.
I tuck myself in a little deeper,
like a coffin resting in its earthen grave.
Buried deep, no longer aware,
I slept fast till the warm rays of morning appeared.

I walked to the house of the Lord today.
Kneeling in prayer, I would seek a vision of the divine plan.
I wished to beg of the blessed Mary, to grant me relief
from my life long grief and endless despair.

The sidewalk pressed down hard with the weight of humanity.
As I trod down Geary Street,
I noticed old man Thomas in his unusual haunt.
Clenching brown bagged whiskey in a withered hand,
his impish grin pierced through a drunkard's abandoned mask.

He cried out to me; "where ya been hiden' honey?
*   Can I get yer somym? I can buy ya a drink...*
*   cuz I'z got money taday!"*
"No, but thanks, I'm o.k."

He described the harsh winds and rains of last night.
He had managed to bury himself inside the entry of an
abandoned store, just 'round the corner from where I reside.

"man dem rains blew hard… but I'z dried out today.
…Gosh where ya been hidin' yerself honey?
He spoke to me as if I were a real friend.

"Tom, I'm goin' over to Saint Anne's Church to pray."

He drifted into a conversation about the war, which one I do not
know, explaining that he unsure of life or death had done some
'bent knee' time. "man, I've prayed to God wit da Jews, da
Catholics and wit dem Jehovahs. When yer dien' it's all da same. I'd
go wit ya but I'z a mess." he said, as he pointed to himself, a bottle
in his left hand, the faint smell of urine emanating from
his chair, layers of tattered clothes, an unshaven face, silvery
blonde hair, uncombed and disheveled.

He did ask me to pray for him though,
spelling carefully his name.
I realized he may have wanted to come with me.
Perhaps he had been rejected before.
Surely not wanting to cause me any grief, he said;
"I'll wait fer ya here, I'll watch fer ya ta come out."
My people, the 'Christed ones,'
had not been kind to my friend on the street.

I commented, as I left Tom positioned as my personal watchman;
"I may not even get in the front door, now a days the doors are
mostly locked." But then I thought, 'it's Sunday, there's a good
chance of getting in.'

I headed across the boulevard, cars madly dashing to and fro.
A roaring voice came up from behind,
frightening me off the center island.
For a brief moment I thought, 'should I fling myself in front of
the oncoming fire truck?'
I grabbed my wrap up tight around me,
feeling that same chill of last night emerging from deep within.
Cautiously, I made my way through two lanes of intermittent traffic.

I looked back, wonder, 'did Thomas feel my delay?'
No, he was looking off down the street.

I resolutely moved toward the sanctuary of Catholics.
Approaching the stairway, I began my assent.
I reached up, almost unconsciously to the pin I had worn with pride.
Removing it from my shirt, so as not to offend the pious,
the button proclaimed, my sexual preference as 'often.'
I slipped it silently into my purse.

I felt a sadness moving in me.
What I sought was old and familiar.
Once I had found solace in
the sacredness of the house of the Lord.

I reached out for the door on the right... Locked.
I stepped to the middle door, I pulled,
then pushed... Locked.
One last door, the door on the left... Locked.

I walked down the steps away from the rejecting doors.
As my feet met the pavement, I remembered to look up.
There he was with the gentle eyes of God,
watching me, as he had promised.
I raised my hand to wave. His hand echoed my salute.

I looked down, pondering the meaning of this.
My mind heard a sweet voice speak to my question;
"We left the churches, didn't you hear?
There was no room for the sick, lonely and discontent,
no room for the homeless, the meek, or even the merciful,"
she whispered.
"These buildings are just the shell of what they could have been.
When you and Thomas share love, my presence is with you.
I would not alienate you my sweet child,
it's only doors and brick.
The house of the Lord is now the love you build
between yourself and every other human being."

Make Room For Me

Make room for me friends.
I'm on my way!
When I finally arrive,
I intend to stay.
So open heaven's gates.
Light the lamps.
The bride is ready,
to marry Christ at long last.

A Mind Unto Myself

No one is wrong when it comes to this thing.
No one can truly be blamed.
People grow apart.
Some of us force them to find deeper truth,
while others are left behind.
They scurry through the traditions they were born into.
Deciding.
Having a mind unto myself is of greatest value to me.

Condemnation Of Souls

I seem to be preoccupied with the condemnation of souls.
Who has the right to say you go or you stay?
Let each soul, rather, to their own creator answer.

Can someone exist with multiple souls?
Each soul vying for top dog position.
Can a person be happy or whole,
if they are fragments of one or another?

Why do some souls choose to share one body?
Might they be working out some karmic debt?
Maybe a more altruistic goal of
helping humanity is part of the grand design.

We Love On Different Levels

Sometimes when I see someone I have not seen in ages,
I burst with love, understanding and appreciation.
I liken it to the sudden blooming of a
grand row of cherry blossoms lining the path.

Confusion

I am confused.
Integration seems impossible.
I have aspects of persona that speak to me.
Yet I am saddled with nightmares.
Dreams of my clan,
a mother, father, brothers and sisters.
During the day I am in love.
At night I am blinded to my waking life.
I can't remember my precious lover.
I experience only vague memories
of the intimacy I share in my waking hours.

I feel insane.
I am like an unmendable piece of luscious fabric.
I am beautiful and useless, unless,
I am cut into pieces to avoid the flaw.
I become a quilt of nightmares and
happy daydreams.

Did I build my treasure on rotten wood
of decaying past?
Is my quest for love and peace impossible?
Should I scream, die or cut?
Am I still mendable or is it too late to be healed?

I Wish I Were A Parakeet

I wish I were a parakeet.
A screeching, cawing, birdling.
Freely soaring with my friends.
My feathered life unfurling.

I Am

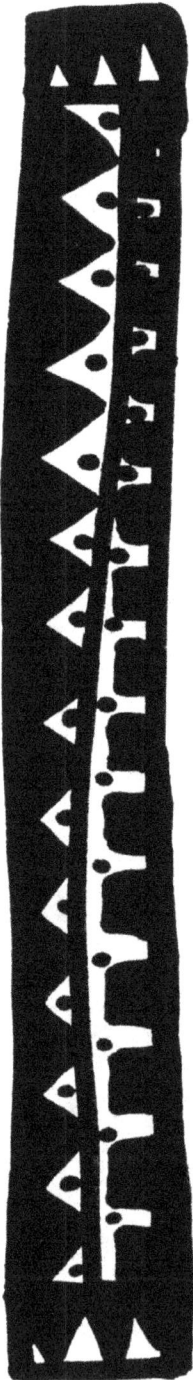

I am the baker, my creations exquisite.
    I am fresh pastry and bread that you eat.
I am the seed, incubating new life.
    I am the farmer, harvesting the crop.
I am creator, maker of life.
    I am created, learning to walk.
I am the cherry, red, round and juicy.
    I am the pit, growing into a tree.
I am the window, glass lit with warm sunshine.
    I am the world, through your windows of time.
I am the singer voicing our pleasure.
    I am the song, free floating in air.
I am a song bird, bold, blue and beautiful.
    I am the chirping that inspires your heart.
I am sheet music, lines, notes and paper.
    I am expressions of divine melodies.
I am a poet scrawling words for my pleasure.
    I am the poem, transcending space and time.
I am the nation, diverse laws and people.
    I am the citizen, crying out to be heard.
I am the war, principals worth a fight.
    I am the young solder, dying tonight.
I am the bombs, innocent and quiet.
    I am explosions, destroying all life.
I am a prison, a fortress of strength.
    I am the murderer, waiting to die.
I am the mother, bearer of children.
    I am the child, seeking my mother of light.
I am the teacher, strict and hard driving.
    I am the student, hungry to learn.
I am the lover caressing and holding.
    I am the beloved, receiving the love.

I am the dancer, sweating and tired.
I am the dance of pelicans in flight.
I am the painter, brushing glazes and varnish.
I am the canvas, brilliant with hues.
I am the weaver with threads, looms and shuttles.
I am the blanket, warming your child.
I am the towel, soft, fluffy and absorbent.
I am the skin, caressed tenderly dry.
I am pain swirling through the infirm.
I am the body struggling to live.
I am the butcher, meat do I render.
I am the calf, slaughtered for ground round.
I am the carpenter, hammering wood stuff.
I am a tree amputated for your use.
I am the Master, my wisdom unending.
I am disciple, hungry to learn.
I am culture, fine clothes and parties.
I am the identity mask, you hide behind.
I am the gardener, planting and pruning.
I am the flowers and herbs that heal life.
I am the sailor, rugged and strong.
I am rocking boat holding you safe.
I am the sail, canvas and seams.
I am the wind blowing magic to your beams.
I am the traveler, crossing the nations.
I am the path in life you must cross.
I am the horse strong dark and lovely.
I am the rider with reins in my hand
I am the pen writing this poem,
I am the I
                    N
                        K…..I want to be done!!

Too Long Have I Lived

Too long have I lived to hope for something different.
I am what I am and have what I've been given.
I won't awake younger or prettier or firmer tomorrow.

The time worn path of age marches through my valley.
I, like a good soldier, march in step to its constant rhythm.

To be young again,
to dream dreams,
know the sweetness of love,
the ecstasy of love's embrace,
to gaze once more on the miracle of new life,
Would I dare to hope for so much?

Perhaps it is not so much,
for I am just nine and thirty.
There is still time for me to look upon future
unknown to me now.

I'm No Quitter

I'm no quitter.
I fight.
But I hate violence.
So it's not.
I stand firm.
I'm a ball of mush inside.
I stay.
As long as it takes.
To my detriment sometimes.
Life happens.
Sometimes it's not a pretty thing.
I've been bruised.
That won't stop me from loving.

Beloved

Beloved, let us love one another.
Love is of God,
everyone who loves is born of God and knows God.

Beloved, let us love one another.

I love.
I love people as they are.

I love Jackie.
At just under ninety pounds,
she is a lovable human being.
Cancer has a grip on her body, but not her soul.
She takes large doses of pain medication
to allow herself the joy of my gentle touch.
I love her body, covered with map like incisions.
I love the flesh holding the patches.
I love the skin that holds a disintegrating body.
Mostly I love her spirit.
I bless her with ancient Sanskrit prayers.
And as she passes,
I love her freed spirit.
I love my own cancer cells.
I die with her passing,
reborn more human, more loving, in my own resurrection.

Inspired by; First John 4:7,8

The Walk

Not far or long,
just a little jaunt,
at the Japanese tea gardens
a favorite haunt.

A flower,
a leaf,
a bug crawling by.

Glorious Buddha
will catch my eye.

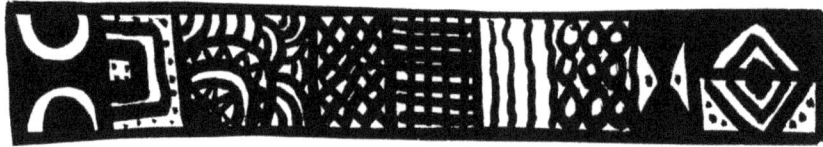

Communion

I give to you my body,
that which was shed for you and for many.

I give to you my physicality, my weakness.

I give to you my body,
raped and beaten for the salvation of those in greater need than I.

I give to you my body,
that has endured endless explorations of surgical bleedings,
destroyed by the oral radiations of treatment.

I give you my body,
a body many covet, yet at times I have found little use for.

I give to you my body,
full of planted seeds, wanted and unwanted.
A field in need of hoeing.
A rich and fertile ground endangered by the insidious power of
grief strickened memorial weeds.

I give to you my body,
starved, drunken and drugged.

I give to you my blood,
blood that flows freely for you and for many for the
remission of sins.

I give to you my blood,
the warm red river that left my veins when torn skin
could no longer hold in the battered child.
Blood puddled in my stockings fearing to leave my life
crumpled on the wooden floor beneath my limp frame.

I give to you my blood,
blood that dances down my legs on the days of my holy time.
Flowing freely from my womb to bless your linguam
with it incredible power.

I give to you my blood,
A crimson flood that drained, each time new life proclaimed.

I give to you my blood,
painfully stolen from my vagina as a vile intruder
robbed me of my purity.

I give to you my blood,
channels of life itself coursing through my veins and arteries.
Blood forcing its way through the prolapsed valves
of my restored heart.

Take and eat. This is my body.
As you take me in, my innocence and my purity live in you.

Take and drink. This is the blood I have spilled for you.
The blood of all the events that have shaped me
into the finest of suppers.

I offer myself to you as a redemption.
I offer you my body and blood to free myself
of this lonely human experience.

I am your salvation.
As you accept me, eat and drink of me freely.

Do this in memory of all who have suffered and are suffering.
Do this in memory of me.

Amen

Inspired by;   Mark 14:22–24
*   Matthew 26:26–27*
*   Luke 22:19–20*

Truth And Illusion

It isn't that I'm bad or good, it's that I'm really nothing.
It isn't that I'm foolish or wise, what's important are the dumb things.
Can I breathe without a sound? Or cry without a tear drop?
Can I hold on with my mind when the beat of my heart has stopped?

What's real is not in question here. Truth is surely wrong.
My view of things is never right because I see too much.
I see the lies and deceptions and agree I have not seen them.
Blindness saves my body from pain of beating and molestations.

When called upon to speak the truth, I must only speak lies.
I am rewarded for calling lies the truth,
punished for revealing the unspeakable truth.
Truth is unpleasant to those in power. Yet they truly are the weakest.
They build their lives on lies. I build my life on truth.

When it comes time to stand and be accounted for,
I will stand on solid ground. I will stand on truth.
They will tumble and crash, having built a life on illusion.
When illusion is no longer accepted in place of accuracy,
what is left?

Truth!

After Thoughts

I wrote this work over the last year, a time of great change, and interaction with many people.

I choose this simple format for my first book, and self-published fifty copies, lovingly hand bound.

I found myself writing with the church or scripture as the theme on occasion. I was trying to resolve for myself the purity and truth I find in the teacher (in this case Jesus Christ) to the dramatic disparity so often seen in churches, synagogues and temples. It was not meant as blasphemy, but rather the cry of a voice in the desert, inquiring and sometimes angry with God's people. We all come from God, and unto Him/Her we shall return.

Self-published
November 1996
San Francisco, CA